Blueprint to Success

Mastering the Art of Business Plans that Win

Jules Beshears

I0479974

Contents

1.

2.

3.

4.

5.

6.

7.

8.

9.

10.

11.

12.

13.

14.

Message From The Author

Iwas told , **"We are paid for our value and not our time."** As such, my books, on the surface, may seem somewhat lacking in terms of page count. What they lack in the sheer number of pages that tell stories about me growing up, or making my first million, etc., I choose to prioritize value. The books I write remove most of the fluff and are condensed, distilled, raw value that will hopefully change your life for the better.

This book is dedicated to my family, friends, and to all the entrepreneurs that chose never to give up.

Chapter 1

Unveiling the Masterplan: The Power of a Winning Business Plan

Every great business begins with a vision, but it takes more than an idea to transform it into reality. The bridge between a dream and a successful enterprise is a well-crafted business plan. In this chapter, we will explore the power of a winning business plan and how it can pave the way to achieving your entrepreneurial aspirations.

A business plan serves as the roadmap for your business, guiding you from its conception to its growth and evolution. It lays out your goals, strategies, and the resources needed to achieve your objectives. The power of a winning business plan lies in its ability to:

1. Provide clarity and direction: A business plan helps you establish a clear vision and mission for your company. It outlines the steps necessary to reach your goals, enabling you to make informed decisions and maintain focus on what truly matters.

2. Attract investors and partners: A compelling business plan can capture the interest of investors, lenders, and potential business partners. It demonstrates your ability to think strategically, identify opportunities, and mitigate risks, thus instilling confidence in your venture's potential for success.

3. Serve as a management tool: A comprehensive business plan allows you to identify key performance indicators (KPIs) and

set benchmarks for progress. By regularly reviewing and updating your plan, you can measure your business's performance and adjust your strategies to ensure continued growth.

4. Identify potential challenges and opportunities: Creating a business plan involves conducting thorough market research and analysis. This process helps you identify potential challenges, competitors, and opportunities, allowing you to develop strategies to address them proactively.

5. Communicate your vision: A well-structured business plan effectively communicates your business's purpose, goals, and strategies to your team, investors, and other stakeholders. It aligns everyone's efforts towards a common objective and fosters a sense of shared ownership in the company's success.

Embarking on the journey of crafting a winning business plan can seem daunting, but with the right guidance and approach, it is an exciting and rewarding process. "Blueprint to Success: Mastering the Art of Business Plans that Win" will provide you with the tools and insights needed to create a compelling, strategic, and actionable plan that sets your business on the path to success.

In the upcoming chapters, we will delve deeper into the essential components of a winning business plan, from refining your unique business idea to securing investments and partnerships. By the end of this book, you will have developed a comprehensive, well-researched, and compelling business plan that will serve as the foundation for your entrepreneurial success story. Let's begin this journey together and unlock the power of a winning business plan.

Chapter 2

The Visionary's Canvas: Crafting Your Unique Business Idea

Transforming your entrepreneurial dream into a reality begins with a unique and viable business idea. In this chapter, we'll guide you through the process of refining your idea and articulating it in a way that sets the stage for the rest of your business plan.

Define Your Passion and Purpose

Your journey starts with identifying the driving force behind your business idea. Ask yourself:

- What are you passionate about?
- What problem or need does your business address?
- How can your products or services improve people's lives or experiences?

By defining the passion and purpose behind your business, you create a solid foundation that will guide and inspire your decisions as you develop your business plan.

Identify Your Target Market

A successful business caters to the needs of a specific group of customers. To pinpoint your target market, consider:

- Who are the people most likely to need or desire your products or services?
- What are their demographics, such as age, gender, income, and location?

- What are their psychographics, such as interests, values, and lifestyles?

Understanding your target market will help you tailor your products, services, and marketing efforts to their preferences and needs.

Analyze Your Competitors

Assessing your competition is crucial to identifying your unique selling proposition (USP) and carving out your niche in the market. To gain a competitive edge, you should:

- Identify direct and indirect competitors in your industry.
- Analyze their strengths and weaknesses, including products, services, pricing, and marketing strategies.
- Determine what sets your business apart from the competition and how you can leverage these differences.

Test and Validate Your Idea

Before diving into the details of your business plan, it's essential to test and validate your business idea. This process may involve:

- Conducting market research to determine the demand for your products or services.
- Creating a minimum viable product (MVP) to gather feedback from potential customers.
- Analyzing customer feedback and adjusting your business idea accordingly.

Validating your idea helps ensure that you're moving forward with a concept that has the potential for success.

Craft a Clear and Compelling Value Proposition

A value proposition is a concise statement that communicates the unique benefits your products or services provide to your target market. Your value proposition should answer the following questions:

- What problem does your business solve, or what need does it fulfill?
- How do your products or services solve this problem or fulfill this need?
- Why should customers choose your business over the competition?

A well-crafted value proposition will serve as the cornerstone of your business plan, guiding your strategies and decisions throughout the planning process.

As you move forward in developing your business plan, keep the insights from this chapter in mind. By crafting a unique business idea, identifying your target market, analyzing your competitors, validating your idea, and creating a compelling value proposition, you'll establish a strong foundation for your business that will set the stage for success. In the next chapter, we'll dive into the essential elements of a compelling business plan, providing you with a roadmap for turning your vision into a thriving enterprise.

Chapter 3

The Nitty-Gritty: Essential Elements of a Compelling Business Plan

A well-crafted business plan is a strategic document that outlines the path to success for your venture. In this chapter, we will cover the essential elements that make up a compelling business plan, providing a comprehensive roadmap for your entrepreneurial journey.

Executive Summary

The executive summary is a concise overview of your entire business plan. It should provide a snapshot of your company, your unique value proposition, your target market, and your financial projections. Although it appears first in the plan, it's often best to write the executive summary last, as it will be a summary of the entire document.

Company Description

The company description offers an in-depth look at your business, its history, and its mission, vision, and values. This section should also cover your business structure, legal considerations, and any unique aspects that set your company apart from the competition.

Market Analysis

A thorough market analysis demonstrates that you understand the industry, the competition, and the needs of your target market. This section should include the following:

- A description of your industry, its size, growth trends, and outlook.
- An analysis of your target market, including demographics, psychographics, and buyer behavior.
- A competitive analysis, highlighting your competitors' strengths and weaknesses and identifying opportunities for your business.

Products and Services

This section should provide a detailed description of your products and services, focusing on the features and benefits that set them apart from the competition. Be sure to emphasize the problem or need that your offerings address and how they fulfill the desires of your target market.

Marketing and Sales Strategy

Your marketing and sales strategy outlines how you plan to reach your target market, generate leads, and convert them into customers. This section should cover:

- Your marketing channels and tactics, such as social media, content marketing, advertising, and public relations.
- Your sales strategy, including your sales process, team structure, and incentives.
- A timeline of marketing and sales activities and key milestones.

Operations Plan

The operations plan details the day-to-day activities required to run your business effectively. This section should cover:

- Your business's location, facilities, and equipment.
- An overview of your production or service delivery process.

- A description of your management team, their roles, and their qualifications.
- Your staffing plan, including employee recruitment, training, and retention strategies.

Financial Projections

The financial projections section is a critical component of your business plan, as it provides an overview of your business's financial health and growth potential. This section should include:

- A sales forecast projecting your revenue for the next three to five years.
- An income statement detailing your projected revenues, expenses, and profits.
- A cash flow statement illustrating how cash will flow in and out of your business.
- A balance sheet showing your business's assets, liabilities, and equity.

Appendix (Optional)

The appendix is an optional section where you can include any supporting documents or additional information that may be relevant to your business plan. This may include resumes of key team members, market research data, product specifications, or legal documents.

By incorporating these essential elements into your business plan, you'll create a comprehensive and strategic document that will guide your business's growth and development. As you work through the remaining chapters of this book, you'll delve deeper into each of these sections, gaining valuable insights and tools to help you craft a winning business plan that sets your venture on the path to success.

Chapter 4

Market Magic: Identifying and Capturing Your Target Audience

Understanding your target audience is a crucial factor in the success of your business. In this chapter, we will explore how to identify and capture your target market by conducting thorough research and developing strategies tailored to their preferences and needs.

Conduct Market Research

Market research involves gathering and analyzing data to understand the preferences, habits, and needs of your target audience. There are two types of market research: primary and secondary.

- Primary research: This involves collecting data directly from your target audience through methods such as surveys, interviews, focus groups, and observations. Primary research can provide insights into customers' opinions, preferences, and buying habits.

- Secondary research: This involves gathering data from existing sources, such as industry reports, market studies, and competitor analyses. Secondary research can help you understand market trends, industry benchmarks, and the competitive landscape.

Develop Customer Personas

Customer personas are fictional representations of your ideal customers based on real data and insights gained from your market research. Creating customer personas can help you:

- Understand your customers' needs, preferences, and motivations.
- Tailor your products, services, and marketing messages to resonate with your target audience.
- Identify the most effective marketing channels and tactics for reaching your customers.

Segment Your Market

Market segmentation involves dividing your target audience into smaller, more specific groups based on shared characteristics. Common segmentation criteria include demographics, geographic location, psychographics, and behavior. By segmenting your market, you can:

- Create tailored marketing strategies for each segment, increasing the effectiveness of your marketing efforts.
- Identify potential niche markets and opportunities for growth.
- Improve customer satisfaction and loyalty by addressing the unique needs and preferences of each segment.

Analyze Your Competition

Understanding your competition is key to identifying opportunities and differentiating your business in the market. To analyze your competitors, consider the following:

- Identify your main competitors and their market share.

- Assess their strengths and weaknesses, including product offerings, pricing, marketing strategies, and customer experience.
- Determine the factors that set your business apart and how you can leverage these differences to gain a competitive edge.

Position Your Brand

Your brand positioning is the unique space your business occupies in the minds of your target audience. To create a compelling brand positioning, consider the following:

- Your unique selling proposition (USP) highlights the features and benefits that set your business apart from the competition.
- Your brand personality defines the tone, style, and voice of your marketing communications.
- Your brand promise, which communicates the value and experience customers can expect from your business.

Develop Your Marketing Strategy

With a deep understanding of your target audience and your brand positioning, you can now develop a marketing strategy tailored to your customer's preferences and needs. Your marketing strategy should include the following:

- Your marketing goals and objectives, such as increasing brand awareness, generating leads, or boosting sales.
- Your marketing tactics and channels, such as social media, email marketing, content marketing, and advertising.
- Your marketing budget and resources, including personnel, tools, and technology.

By identifying and capturing your target audience through market research, customer personas, segmentation, competitive analysis, and brand positioning, you'll lay the groundwork for a successful marketing strategy that drives results. In the next chapter, we'll dive into analyzing your business rivals and standing out in the market, helping you further refine your business plan and secure your competitive   advantage.

Chapter 5

Outshining the Competition: Analyzing Rivals and Standing Out in the Market

In a competitive business landscape, understanding your rivals and differentiating your business is essential to success. In this chapter, we'll explore how to analyze your competition, identify your unique selling proposition, and stand out in the market.

Conduct a Competitive Analysis

A competitive analysis is a systematic evaluation of your competitor's strengths and weaknesses. To conduct a comprehensive competitive analysis, follow these steps:

- Identify your main competitors, including direct and indirect rivals.
- Assess their market share, product offerings, pricing strategies, customer experience, and marketing efforts.
- Examine their online presence, including websites, social media, and customer reviews.
- Analyze their strengths and weaknesses to uncover opportunities for your business.

Identify Your Unique Selling Proposition (USP)

Your USP is the distinctive combination of features, benefits, and values that sets your business apart from the competition. To identify your USP, consider:

- The problem or need your business addresses and how your products or services provide a solution.

- The unique features or benefits of your products or services make them stand out from competitors.
- The aspects of your business that resonate most strongly with your target audience, such as exceptional customer service, superior quality, or competitive pricing.

Leverage Your Competitive Advantage

Once you've identified your USP, it's time to leverage your competitive advantage to stand out in the market. You can do this by:

- Highlighting your USP in your marketing messages, ensuring that your target audience understands the unique value your business provides.
- Continuously improving and innovating your products or services to stay ahead of the competition.
- Focusing on customer satisfaction and building strong relationships with your customers to encourage loyalty and word-of-mouth referrals.

Monitor Your Competition

The business landscape is constantly evolving, and staying ahead of your competition requires ongoing vigilance. Regularly monitoring your competitors can help you:

- Stay informed about new products, services, or marketing strategies they launch.
- Identify emerging trends or shifts in customer preferences.
- Adapt and refine your strategies to maintain your competitive edge.

Embrace Collaboration

While competition is inevitable, it's also essential to recognize opportunities for collaboration. Partnering with complementary businesses can help you:

- Reach new customers and expand your market reach.
- Combine resources and expertise to create innovative products or services.
- Learn from your competitors' experiences and adopt best practices.

By analyzing your competition, identifying your USP, leveraging your competitive advantage, and embracing collaboration, you'll position your business to outshine the competition and capture a larger share of the market. In the next chapter, we'll delve into the process of creating a powerful marketing and sales strategy that will help you reach your target audience, generate leads, and convert them into loyal customers.

Chapter 6

Mastering the Art of Attraction: Crafting a Winning Marketing and Sales Strategy

A successful marketing and sales strategy is the key to attracting and converting customers, driving growth, and establishing your brand in the market. In this chapter, we'll guide you through the process of crafting a winning marketing and sales strategy tailored to your target audience.

Set Clear Marketing Objectives

Your marketing objectives should be specific, measurable, achievable, relevant, and time-bound (SMART). These objectives include increasing brand awareness, generating leads, boosting sales, and improving customer retention. Establishing clear objectives will help you focus your marketing efforts and measure your success.

Choose the Right Marketing Channels

Select the most effective marketing channels for reaching your target audience based on their preferences, habits, and demographics. Common marketing channels include:

- Social media platforms, such as Facebook, Instagram, Twitter, and LinkedIn.
- Content marketing, including blog posts, articles, videos, podcasts, and e-books.
- Email marketing, using targeted campaigns to engage and nurture leads.

- Search engine optimization (SEO) is optimizing your website to rank higher in search results.
- Paid advertising, such as Google Ads, Facebook Ads, and sponsored content.

Create Compelling Content

Develop engaging, informative, and persuasive content tailored to your target audience and aligned with your brand positioning. Your content should address your customer's needs, provide solutions to their problems, and demonstrate the value of your products or services.

Implement a Lead Generation Strategy

Lead generation is the process of attracting and converting prospects into potential customers. To generate leads, consider the following:

- Offering valuable content or resources, such as e-books, whitepapers, or webinars, in exchange for contact information.
- Hosting events, workshops, or networking opportunities to connect with your target audience.
- Using social media and online advertising to drive targeted traffic to your website or landing pages.

Develop a Sales Process

A structured sales process is essential to efficiently converting leads into customers. Your sales process might include:

- Qualifying leads based on their fit for your products or services.
- Nurturing relationships with prospects through email campaigns, phone calls, or personalized content.

- Presenting tailored sales pitches or product demonstrations to showcase the value of your offerings.
- Overcoming objections and addressing concerns to close the deal.

Measure and Optimize Your Strategy

Regularly tracking and analyzing the performance of your marketing and sales efforts is crucial to continuous improvement. Monitor key performance indicators (KPIs) such as website traffic, lead conversion rates, and sales revenue to assess your progress toward your objectives. Use this data to identify areas for improvement and optimize your strategy accordingly.

By crafting a winning marketing and sales strategy tailored to your target audience, you'll be well-equipped to attract and convert customers, drive growth, and establish your brand in the market. In the next chapter, we'll explore the operational aspects of running a successful business, including managing your team, production processes, and day-to-day activities.

Chapter 7

Operational Excellence: Streamlining Your Business for Success

Efficient operations are the backbone of a successful business. In this chapter, we'll explore the key aspects of managing your day-to-day activities, streamlining production processes, and building a high-performing team.

Optimize Your Production or Service Delivery Process

An efficient production or service delivery process ensures you can meet customer demand while maintaining high quality and minimizing costs. To optimize your process, consider:

- Identifying and eliminating bottlenecks or inefficiencies.
- Adopting lean production principles to minimize waste and improve productivity.
- Implementing process automation or technology solutions where appropriate.

Manage Your Supply Chain

An effective supply chain ensures the timely delivery of raw materials, products, and services. To manage your supply chain, consider:

- Developing strong relationships with suppliers and negotiating favorable terms.
- Implementing inventory management systems to track stock levels and prevent shortages.

- Establishing contingency plans to address potential disruptions or delays.

Build a Strong Management Team

A competent management team is essential to guide your business's growth and development. To build a strong management team, consider:

- Hiring experienced managers with a track record of success in your industry.
- Providing ongoing training and development opportunities to enhance their skills.
- Clearly defining roles and responsibilities to ensure accountability and effective decision-making.

Develop a Comprehensive Staffing Plan

Your staffing plan should outline your human resource needs, including the number of employees required, their roles, and the skills they need to possess. To develop a comprehensive staffing plan, consider the following:

- Assessing your current workforce and identifying gaps or areas for improvement.
- Developing job descriptions and hiring criteria for each position.
- Implementing recruitment and selection processes to attract and retain top talent.

Foster a Positive Work Culture

A positive work culture promotes employee engagement, satisfaction, and productivity. To foster a positive work culture, consider:

- Encouraging open communication and collaboration among team members.
- Providing regular feedback and recognition to acknowledge employees' efforts and achievements.
- Offering a supportive environment that promotes work-life balance and employee well-being.

Implement Financial Controls and Reporting Systems

Effective financial management is critical to maintaining your business's financial health and ensuring profitability. To implement financial controls and reporting systems, consider:

- Establishing budgets and financial targets for each department or project.
- Implementing accounting software or systems to track revenues, expenses, and cash flow.
- Regularly reviewing financial reports to monitor performance and identify areas for improvement.

By streamlining your business operations, optimizing your production or service delivery processes, and building a high-performing team, you'll set your business on the path to success. In the final chapter, we'll discuss the importance of financial projections and how to create a solid financial plan to support your business's growth and stability.

Chapter 8

Financial Forecasting Mastery: Navigating the Road to Sustainable Growth

Financial projections play a crucial role in planning and managing your business's growth and stability. In this chapter, we will delve into the process of creating a comprehensive financial plan, including the key components of financial projections, understanding cash flow management, and developing strategies to ensure your business's financial success.

The Importance of Financial Projections

Financial projections are estimates of your business's future financial performance, including revenues, expenses, and profitability. Accurate financial projections are essential for:

- Securing funding from investors or lenders requires a clear understanding of your business's potential for growth and profitability.
- Guiding strategic decision-making by helping you assess the financial impact of various business scenarios and opportunities.
- Monitoring your business's financial health and identifying potential issues or areas for improvement.

Key Components of Financial Projections

A comprehensive financial plan should include the following components:

- Sales forecast An estimate of your future sales revenues based on factors such as market trends, customer demand, and your marketing and sales strategies.
- Income statement: A summary of your business's revenues and expenses over a specific period, showing your net income or loss.
- Cash flow statement: A record of your business's cash inflows and outflows, providing insight into your liquidity and ability to meet financial obligations.
- Balance sheet: A snapshot of your business's financial position at a specific point in time, detailing your assets, liabilities, and equity.
- Breakeven analysis: The point at which your revenues equal your expenses, indicating the minimum sales volume required to cover your costs.

Developing Accurate Financial Projections

To create accurate financial projections, follow these steps:

- Conduct thorough market research to gather data on industry trends, customer demand, and competitor performance.
- Use historical financial data from your business or similar businesses in your industry as a starting point for your projections.
- Consider various scenarios and assumptions, including best-case, worst-case, and most likely outcomes.
- Regularly review and update your projections based on new information, market developments, or changes in your business strategy.

Understanding Cash Flow Management

Effective cash flow management is essential to ensure your business has sufficient funds to cover its expenses and support its growth. To manage your cash flow, consider:

- Developing a cash flow budget to forecast your expected cash inflows and outflows over a specific period.
- Implementing strategies to increase cash inflows, such as offering discounts for early payments, diversifying your income streams, or expanding your customer base.
- Minimizing cash outflows by reducing expenses, negotiating favorable payment terms with suppliers, or improving inventory management.
- Establishing a cash reserve or line of credit to cover unexpected expenses or cash shortfalls.

Monitoring and Measuring Financial Performance

Regularly monitoring your financial performance helps you assess your progress toward your financial goals and identify potential issues or areas for improvement. To monitor and measure your financial performance, consider:

- Tracking key financial metrics, such as gross profit margin, net profit margin, and return on investment (ROI).
- Comparing your actual financial results against your projections to identify variances and adjust your strategies accordingly.
- Conducting regular financial audits to ensure the accuracy and reliability of your financial data.

Developing Financial Strategies for Sustainable Growth

To ensure your business's financial success and sustainable growth, consider developing and implementing the following strategies:

- Diversify your revenue streams to reduce reliance on a single product, service, or customer segment.
- Optimize your pricing strategy to maximize profitability while maintaining competitiveness in the market.
- Implement cost-saving measures to improve efficiency and reduce expenses, such as automating processes, outsourcing non-core tasks, or renegotiating supplier contracts.

Seek external funding sources, such as loans, grants, or investments, to support your growth initiatives and provide additional financial resources.

Adapting Your Financial Plan to Changing Business Conditions

The business environment is dynamic, and your financial plan should be flexible enough to adapt to changing conditions. To ensure your financial plan remains relevant and effective, consider the following:

- Continuously monitoring market trends, economic indicators, and competitor activities to identify potential opportunities or challenges.
- Revising your financial projections and strategies based on new information, such as changes in customer demand, cost structures, or regulatory requirements.

- Regularly review your financial performance and adjust your goals and targets to reflect your business's evolving needs and priorities.

Communicating Your Financial Plan to Stakeholders

Effectively communicating your financial plan to key stakeholders, such as investors, lenders, employees, and business partners, is essential to gain their support and trust. To communicate your financial plan effectively, consider the following:

- Clearly explaining the rationale behind your financial projections and assumptions, using data and evidence to support your claims.
- Highlighting the potential benefits and returns on investment (ROI) for stakeholders, such as increased profits, market share, or customer satisfaction.
- Addressing any concerns or questions stakeholders may have regarding your financial plan and demonstrating your commitment to transparency and accountability.

By creating a comprehensive financial plan, understanding cash flow management, monitoring your financial performance, and developing strategies for sustainable growth, you'll ensure your business's financial success and stability. With a solid financial foundation in place, you'll be well-equipped to navigate the challenges and opportunities that lie ahead on the road to business success.

- In conclusion, this book has provided you with a step-by-step guide to creating a successful business plan, covering topics such as market analysis, competitive positioning, marketing and sales strategies, operational excellence, and financial planning. By following the advice and recommendations presented in these chapters, you'll be well on your way to launching and growing a thriving business that stands out in today's competitive marketplace.

Chapter 9

Scaling New Heights: Strategies for Long-Term Business Growth and Success

In this chapter, we'll delve into the strategies and practices that can help you achieve long-term business growth and success. From fostering innovation and embracing digital transformation to building a customer-centric organization and engaging in continuous learning, these strategies will equip you with the tools and insights needed to scale new heights in your business journey.

Foster Innovation and Creativity

Innovation is the lifeblood of business growth and success. To cultivate a culture of innovation and creativity in your organization, consider:

- Encouraging experimentation and risk-taking while recognizing that failure is an integral part of the innovation process.
- Providing resources, tools, and training to support employees in developing new ideas and solutions.
- Establishing processes and platforms for idea-sharing and collaboration, both within your organization and with external partners.

Embrace Digital Transformation

Digital transformation is the integration of digital technologies into all aspects of a business, fundamentally changing how it operates and delivers value to customers. To embrace digital transformation, consider the following:

- Assessing your organization's digital maturity and identifying areas for improvement, such as customer experience, operations, or workforce capabilities.
- Investing in the right technologies, platforms, and tools to streamline processes, enhance productivity, and improve decision-making.
- Developing a digital-first mindset across your organization, including fostering digital literacy, agility, and collaboration.

Build a Customer-Centric Organization

A customer-centric organization focuses on creating and delivering exceptional customer experiences. To build a customer-centric organization, consider:

- Developing a deep understanding of your customer's needs, preferences, and expectations using data, analytics, and customer feedback.
- Designing products, services, and experiences that cater to your customer's unique requirements and deliver superior value.
- Implementing customer-centric processes and policies, such as customer service standards, satisfaction measurement, and continuous improvement initiatives.

Leverage Strategic Partnerships and Collaborations

Strategic partnerships and collaborations can help you access new markets, resources, and capabilities, accelerating your business growth. To leverage strategic partnerships, consider the following:

- Identifying potential partners that share your vision and goals and complement your strengths and weaknesses.

- Establishing clear objectives, expectations, and success metrics for each partnership, ensuring alignment and mutual benefit.
- Investing in relationship-building and communication to foster trust, collaboration, and long-term success.

Engage in Continuous Learning and Improvement

Continuous learning and improvement are essential for staying ahead of the competition and adapting to a constantly changing business environment. To engage in continuous learning and improvement, consider:

- Encouraging a learning mindset within your organization, promoting curiosity, reflection, and growth.
- Providing opportunities for employees to acquire new skills and knowledge, such as training programs, workshops, or mentorship schemes.
- Regularly reviewing and refine your business processes, strategies, and operations, using data, feedback, and benchmarking to drive improvement.

Develop a Robust Risk Management Framework

Effective risk management helps you identify, assess, and mitigate potential threats to your business's growth and success. To develop a robust risk management framework, consider:

- Establishing a dedicated risk management function with clearly defined roles and responsibilities.
- Implementing a systematic risk identification and assessment process using tools such as risk registers, heat maps, and scenario analysis.

- Developing risk mitigation and response strategies, including contingency plans, insurance, and business continuity measures.

Prioritize Sustainability and Social Responsibility

Sustainability and social responsibility are increasingly important drivers of business growth and success, influencing customer preferences, investor decisions, and regulatory requirements. To prioritize sustainability and social responsibility, consider:

- Assessing your organization's environmental, social, and governance (ESG) performance and identifying areas for improvement.

Integrating sustainability and social responsibility into your business strategy, decision-making, and operations, with clear goals and targets.

- Engaging stakeholders, such as employees, customers, suppliers, and communities, in your sustainability and social responsibility initiatives, fosters collaboration and shared value creation.

Cultivate a Strong Organizational Culture

A strong organizational culture promotes employee engagement, satisfaction, and performance, contributing to your business's growth and success. To cultivate a strong organizational culture, consider:

- Defining and communicating your organization's core values, vision, and mission, providing a clear sense of purpose and direction.
- Recognizing and rewarding employees who embody your organization's values and contribute to its success.

- Promoting diversity, inclusion, and equity within your organization, ensuring all employees feel valued, respected, and supported.

Maintain Financial Discipline and Resilience

Financial discipline and resilience are critical for managing your business's growth and navigating economic fluctuations or unforeseen challenges. To maintain financial discipline and resilience, consider the following:

- Implementing robust financial controls and reporting systems to monitor and manage your revenues, expenses, and cash flow.
- Developing a proactive approach to financial planning and forecasting, using scenario analysis and stress testing to assess your business's vulnerability to potential risks.
- Maintaining a healthy balance sheet, with a prudent mix of debt and equity financing and adequate cash reserves or access to credit.

Monitor and Adapt to Industry Trends and Disruptions

Staying abreast of industry trends and disruptions enables you to identify and capitalize on new opportunities and challenges. To monitor and adapt to industry trends and disruptions, consider:

- Regularly analyzing market data, research reports, and news sources to stay informed about emerging trends, technologies, and business models.
- Participating in industry events, conferences, and networking groups, to learn from peers, thought leaders, and influencers.

- Experiment with new ideas, products, or services, and be prepared to pivot your business strategy or operations in response to changing market conditions.
- By implementing these strategies for long-term business growth and success, you'll be better prepared to navigate the complexities of today's dynamic business environment and scale new heights in your entrepreneurial journey. Remember that business success is not a destination, but an ongoing process of learning, adapting and growing. As you continue to develop and refine your business plan, always keep an eye on the horizon, and never lose sight of the passion and purpose that inspired you to embark on this exciting adventure.

Chapter 10

Unleashing the Power of Data: Harnessing Analytics and Business Intelligence for Competitive Advantage

In today's data-driven world, businesses that effectively leverage data, analytics, and business intelligence can gain a significant competitive advantage. In this chapter, we will explore the transformative power of data and how you can harness it to drive better decision-making, enhance operational efficiency, and fuel your business's growth and success.

The Importance of Data-Driven Decision-Making

Data-driven decision-making involves using data and insights to guide your business strategy, operations, and performance management. By adopting a data-driven approach, you can:

- Make more informed and objective decisions, reducing the reliance on intuition, bias, or guesswork.
- Identify trends, patterns, and opportunities that may not be apparent through traditional methods of analysis.
- Monitor and measure the effectiveness of your strategies and initiatives, enabling you to continuously refine and optimize your efforts.

The Building Blocks of a Data-Driven Organization

To become a data-driven organization, you need to establish a strong foundation that includes the following building blocks:

- Data infrastructure: The systems, tools, and technologies that enable you to collect, store, process, and analyze large volumes of data from various sources.
- Data governance: The policies, processes, and standards that ensure the quality, accuracy, security, and compliance of your data.
- Data culture: The mindset, behaviors, and skills that promote data literacy, curiosity, and data-driven decision-making across your organization.

Harnessing Analytics and Business Intelligence

Analytics and business intelligence (BI) involve using advanced tools, techniques, and methodologies to analyze data and derive actionable insights. To harness the power of analytics and BI, consider the following:

- Identifying the key questions, challenges, and opportunities that you want to address through analytics, such as market segmentation, customer behavior, or operational efficiency.
- Selecting the appropriate analytics tools and techniques, such as descriptive, diagnostic, predictive, or prescriptive analytics, depending on your objectives and data availability.
- Developing an analytics roadmap, outlining the steps, resources, and milestones required to implement your analytics initiatives.

Implementing Data-Driven Strategies and Initiatives

Once you have established a solid data foundation and harnessed the power of analytics and BI, you can begin implementing data-driven strategies and initiatives, such as:

- Personalization: Customizing your products, services, and marketing messages to cater to individual customer preferences and behaviors using data and insights.
- Customer journey optimization: Analyzing and mapping your customers' interactions with your brand, identifying pain points, and enhancing their overall experience.
- Process automation and optimization: Using data and analytics to identify inefficiencies in your operations and implementing automation or process improvements to streamline workflows and reduce costs.

Measuring the Impact of Data-Driven Initiatives

To ensure the success of your data-driven initiatives, it is crucial to measure their impact on your business performance and outcomes. Consider:

- Establishing key performance indicators (KPIs) and success metrics, such as revenue growth, customer satisfaction, or operational efficiency.
- Monitoring and reporting on your progress towards your KPIs and targets using dashboards, scorecards, or other visualization tools.
- Conducting regular reviews and evaluations to assess the effectiveness of your initiatives and identify areas for improvement or optimization.

Addressing the Challenges and Risks of Data-Driven Transformation

Becoming a data-driven organization can be a complex and challenging journey, with potential risks and pitfalls along the way. To address these challenges and risks, consider:

- Ensuring compliance with data protection and privacy regulations, such as the General Data Protection Regulation (GDPR), by implementing robust data security and privacy measures.

Addressing data quality and accuracy issues through data cleansing, validation, and enrichment processes, as well as fostering a culture of data stewardship across your organization.

- Managing the ethical and social implications of data-driven decision-making, such as potential biases or discrimination, by establishing ethical guidelines and principles for data usage and analytics.

Building a Data-Driven Workforce

A data-driven workforce is essential for unlocking the full potential of your data and analytics initiatives. To build a data-driven workforce, consider:

- Developing a comprehensive data literacy program, providing training and resources to help employees understand, analyze, and use data in their daily work.

- Encouraging cross-functional collaboration and knowledge-sharing to foster a collective understanding and appreciation of the value of data and analytics.

- Identifying and nurturing data champions and ambassadors within your organization who can promote and support data-driven initiatives and culture.

Staying Ahead of Emerging Data Trends and Technologies

The data landscape is constantly evolving, with new trends, technologies, and opportunities emerging at a rapid pace. To stay ahead of the curve, consider the following:

- Regularly monitoring industry news, research, and events to stay informed about the latest developments in data, analytics, and business intelligence.

- Experiment with new data sources, such as social media, Internet of Things (IoT) devices, or open data, to gain fresh insights and perspectives.

- Exploring advanced analytics techniques, such as artificial intelligence (AI), machine learning, or natural language processing, enhances your analytical capabilities and drives innovation.

Embracing a data-driven approach to business can lead to significant competitive advantages, unlocking new opportunities for growth and success. By following the strategies and recommendations outlined in this chapter, you will be well on your way to harnessing the power of data, analytics, and business intelligence to transform your organization and achieve long-term success.

- As we close this book, remember that creating and executing a successful business plan is a continuous process of learning, adapting, and refining. The insights and guidance provided in these chapters should serve as a valuable resource and roadmap for your entrepreneurial journey. Keep pushing forward, stay resilient, and always be open to new ideas and perspectives.

Your passion, dedication, and hard work will ultimately pave the way for your business's growth and success.

Chapter 11

Nurturing a High-Performance Team: Building and Empowering Your Dream Team for Business Success

In this chapter, we will explore the importance of assembling and nurturing a high-performance team to drive your business's growth and success. From hiring top talent and developing a strong company culture to fostering collaboration and empowering your team members, these strategies will help you build and support an exceptional team that achieves extraordinary results.

The Power of High-Performance Teams

High-performance teams possess a unique combination of skills, motivation, and collaboration that enables them to achieve exceptional results. By building and nurturing a high-performance team, you can:

- Accelerate your business's growth and success by harnessing the collective intelligence, creativity, and expertise of your team members.

- Enhance your organization's adaptability and resilience, empowering your team to navigate challenges and capitalize on opportunities.

- Attract and retain top talent, building a strong employer brand and reputation.

Hiring Top Talent: Finding the Right People for Your Team

Attracting top talent is a critical first step in building your high-performance team. To hire the right people for your team, consider the following:

- Developing clear and compelling job descriptions that outline the skills, experience, and attributes you are seeking in your ideal candidates.
- Leveraging your network, social media, and online job platforms to reach a diverse and talented pool of potential candidates.
- Implementing a structured and objective recruitment process, using techniques such as competency-based interviews, assessments, and reference checks to evaluate candidates' suitability.

Cultivating a Strong Company Culture

A strong company culture can foster employee engagement, satisfaction, and performance, contributing to your team's success. To cultivate a strong company culture, consider:

- Defining and communicating your organization's core values, vision, and mission, providing a clear sense of purpose and direction.
- Recognizing and rewarding employees who embody your organization's values and contribute to its success.
- Promoting diversity, inclusion, and equity within your organization, ensuring all employees feel valued, respected, and supported.

Developing and Retaining Your Team Members

Investing in the professional development and growth of your team members is essential for nurturing a high-performance team. To develop and retain your team members, consider:

- Providing opportunities for employees to acquire new skills and knowledge, such as training programs, workshops, or mentorship schemes.
- Implementing a regular performance review and feedback process, helping employees identify their strengths, areas for improvement, and career goals.
- Offering competitive compensation, benefits, and incentives, such as flexible working arrangements, health and wellness programs, or professional development support.

Fostering Collaboration and Teamwork

Collaboration and teamwork are the hallmarks of high-performance teams, enabling them to harness the collective expertise, creativity, and problem-solving capabilities of their members. To foster collaboration and teamwork, consider the following:

- Encouraging open communication and information-sharing through tools such as team meetings, project management platforms, or internal social networks.
- Implementing team-building activities and initiatives, such as workshops, off-site retreats, or social events, to strengthen relationships and trust among team members.
- Establishing clear roles, responsibilities, and expectations for each team member, ensuring alignment and accountability.

Empowering Your Team Members

Empowering your team members to take ownership of their work and make decisions can lead to increased motivation, engagement, and performance. To empower your team members, consider:

- Delegating responsibility and authority, providing team members with the autonomy and resources they need to achieve their goals.
- Encouraging initiative and innovation, recognizing and rewarding team members who demonstrate leadership and drive positive change.

Providing regular feedback and support, helping team members overcome challenges, learn from their experiences, and grow in their roles.

Managing Conflict and Addressing Performance Issues

Conflict and performance issues can arise in any team, but effective management and resolution are crucial for maintaining a high-performance environment. To manage conflict and address performance issues, consider the following:

- Encouraging open and constructive communication, creating a safe space for team members to share their concerns, feelings, and perspectives.
- Mediating conflicts and facilitating collaborative problem-solving, helping team members find mutually acceptable solutions.
- Providing constructive feedback and coaching for underperforming team members, identifying root causes, and developing action plans for improvement.

Measuring Team Performance and Success

To ensure the ongoing success of your high-performance team, it is essential to measure and evaluate its performance against your business objectives and goals. Consider:

- Establishing team performance indicators and success metrics, such as productivity, quality, customer satisfaction, or innovation.
- Monitoring and reporting on your team's progress toward its performance targets using dashboards, scorecards, or other visualization tools.
- Conducting regular team reviews and evaluations, celebrating successes, identifying areas for improvement, and adjusting your strategies as needed.

Navigating Change and Growth

As your business grows and evolves, your high-performance team may need to adapt and expand to meet new challenges and opportunities. To navigate change and growth, consider:

- Anticipating and planning for future team needs, such as new roles, skills, or resources, based on your business's strategic objectives and growth plans.
- Implementing a structured and inclusive change management process, involving team members in decision-making, and ensuring clear communication and support.
- Encouraging continuous learning and adaptation, fostering a growth mindset and resilience among your team members.

Building a High-Performance Leadership Team

A high-performance leadership team can set the tone for your entire organization, inspiring and guiding your employees toward exceptional results. To build a high-performance leadership team, consider the following:

- Recruiting and developing leaders who embody your organization's values, vision, and mission and possess strong strategic, managerial, and interpersonal skills.
- Investing in leadership development programs, such as executive coaching, leadership workshops, or peer learning groups, to enhance your leaders' capabilities and effectiveness.
- Encouraging collaboration, transparency, and accountability among your leadership team fosters a culture of shared responsibility and collective success.

In conclusion, nurturing a high-performance team is a vital component of your business's long-term growth and success. By following the strategies and recommendations outlined in this chapter, you will be well on your way to building and empowering an extraordinary team that achieves extraordinary results.

- As this book comes to an end, always remember that the journey of entrepreneurship is a continuous process of learning, adapting, and refining. Use the insights and guidance provided in these chapters as a valuable resource and roadmap for your entrepreneurial journey. Keep pushing forward, remain resilient, and stay open to new ideas and perspectives. Your passion, dedication, and hard work will ultimately pave the way for your business's growth and success.

Chapter 12

Achieving Long-Term Success: Cultivating Resilience, Adaptability, and Continuous Improvement in Your Business

In this final chapter, we will explore the key principles and strategies that can help you achieve long-term success in your business. By cultivating resilience, adaptability, and a mindset of continuous improvement, you can navigate the challenges and uncertainties of entrepreneurship and steer your business toward sustainable growth and prosperity.

The Importance of Resilience in Entrepreneurship

Resilience is the ability to withstand adversity, bounce back from setbacks, and persevere through difficult circumstances. In the context of entrepreneurship, resilience is essential for:

- Overcoming the inevitable obstacles, failures, and disappointments that can arise on your entrepreneurial journey.
- Maintaining your motivation, self-confidence, and emotional well-being in the face of stress, uncertainty, and criticism.
- Ensuring the survival and sustainability of your business during challenging economic or market conditions.

Building Personal Resilience as an Entrepreneur

To cultivate resilience as an entrepreneur, consider adopting the following strategies and practices:

- Developing a strong support network of family, friends, mentors, and fellow entrepreneurs who can provide encouragement, advice, and perspective during difficult times.
- Practicing self-compassion and self-care, acknowledging your feelings, and prioritizing your physical, mental, and emotional well-being.
- Embracing a growth mindset, viewing setbacks and failures as opportunities to learn, grow, and become stronger.

Fostering Resilience in Your Business

In addition to building personal resilience, it is crucial to foster resilience within your business, ensuring its capacity to withstand and recover from external shocks or disruptions. To foster resilience in your business, consider the following:

- Diversifying your revenue streams, products, services, or markets to reduce your reliance on any single source of income or demand.
- Implementing robust risk management and contingency planning processes, identifying potential threats to your business, and developing strategies to mitigate their impact.
- Investing in the development and well-being of your employees, cultivating a resilient and adaptable workforce that can navigate change and uncertainty.

The Power of Adaptability in Entrepreneurship

Adaptability is the ability to respond effectively to changing circumstances, seize new opportunities, and innovate in the face of uncertainty. In the context of entrepreneurship, adaptability is crucial for:

- Capitalizing on emerging trends, technologies, and market opportunities that can drive your business's growth and success.
- Navigating changes in your industry, competitive landscape, or customer preferences ensures your business remains relevant and competitive.
- Enhancing your business's agility and responsiveness enables it to pivot, evolve, or reinvent itself as needed.

Cultivating Adaptability in Your Business

To cultivate adaptability in your business, consider implementing the following strategies and practices:

- Encouraging a culture of innovation and experimentation, providing opportunities for employees to explore new ideas, technologies, or business models.
- Monitoring your external environment and staying informed about the latest developments in your industry, market, and competitive landscape.
- Adopting a flexible and iterative approach to strategy and decision-making allowing your business to evolve and adapt its plans and priorities based on new information or insights.

The Mindset of Continuous Improvement

Continuous improvement is the ongoing pursuit of excellence and growth through a process of learning, reflection, and refinement. By adopting a mindset of continuous improvement, you can:

- Enhance the performance and efficiency of your business, identifying and addressing areas of weakness or opportunity.
- Foster a culture of learning and development, empowering your employees to acquire new skills, knowledge, and capabilities.

- Ensure the long-term sustainability and success of your business by continuously striving to exceed your customers' expectations and outperform your competitors.

Implementing Continuous Improvement in Your Business

To implement continuous improvement in your business, consider adopting the following strategies and practices:

- Establishing a regular process of performance measurement, monitoring, and analysis, using key performance indicators (KPIs), benchmarks, or other metrics to track your progress toward your goals.
- Conducting periodic reviews and evaluations of your business processes, systems, and practices, identifying areas for improvement, and implementing corrective actions.
- Encouraging feedback, suggestions, and learning from all members of your organization fosters a culture of open communication and collective growth.

The Role of Customer Feedback and Insights

Customer feedback and insights are invaluable for driving continuous improvement and ensuring your business remains aligned with the needs and expectations of its target audience. To leverage customer feedback and insights for continuous improvement, consider the following:

- Implement regular customer surveys, interviews, or focus groups to gather feedback on your products, services, and overall customer experience.

- Monitoring online reviews, social media conversations, and other sources of customer sentiment, identifying trends, patterns, or areas of concern.

- Acting on customer feedback and insights, prioritizing and implementing changes or improvements that address your customers' needs and concerns.

Learning from Competitors and Best Practices

Benchmarking your business against its competitors and industry best practices can provide valuable insights and inspiration for continuous improvement. To learn from competitors and best practices, consider:

- Conducting competitive analysis, identifying the strengths, weaknesses, opportunities, and threats of your key competitors, and assessing your relative position in the market.

- Researching and adopting industry best practices, standards, or methodologies that can enhance your business's performance, efficiency, or competitiveness.

- Participating in industry events, conferences, or networking groups, sharing knowledge, and learning from the experiences and perspectives of your peers.

Embracing Change and Nurturing a Growth Mindset

Ultimately, achieving long-term success in your business requires embracing change and nurturing a growth mindset among yourself and your team members. To embrace change and nurture a growth mindset, consider:

- Celebrating and rewarding learning, growth, and improvement, recognizing the efforts and achievements of your employees, and fostering a culture of continuous development.
- Encouraging experimentation, risk-taking, and learning from failure, providing a supportive and safe environment for your team to explore new ideas, approaches, and opportunities.
- Continuously challenge and stretch yourself and your team, setting ambitious goals and targets that inspire and motivate everyone to reach their full potential.

In conclusion, cultivating resilience, adaptability, and a mindset of continuous improvement are essential principles for achieving long-term success in your business. By following the strategies and recommendations outlined in this chapter, you can navigate the challenges and uncertainties of entrepreneurship and steer your business toward sustainable growth and prosperity.

As we conclude this book, remember that the journey of entrepreneurship is a continuous process of learning, adapting, and refining. Use the insights and guidance provided in these chapters as a valuable resource and roadmap for your entrepreneurial journey. Keep pushing forward, remain resilient, and stay open to new ideas and perspectives. Your passion, dedication, and hard work will ultimately pave the way for your business's growth and success.

Chapter 13

Bonus Chapter: Mastering the Art of Networking: Expanding Your Circle of Influence and Opportunities

In this bonus chapter, we will delve into the art of networking and how it can play a pivotal role in your entrepreneurial journey. By building and maintaining a strong professional network, you can expand your circle of influence, access valuable resources, and uncover new opportunities for your business.

The Power of Networking in Entrepreneurship

Networking can provide numerous benefits for entrepreneurs, including:

- Access to valuable advice, insights, and expertise from experienced professionals and industry peers.
- Opportunities to form strategic partnerships, collaborations, or joint ventures that can enhance your business's growth and success.
- Increased visibility and credibility for your business, brand, or personal reputation, helping you attract new customers, investors, or talent.

Building Your Professional Network: Where to Start

To build your professional network, consider the following strategies:

- Leverage your existing contacts, such as friends, family, colleagues, or alumni, and ask for introductions or referrals to their professional connections.
- Attend industry events, conferences, workshops, or networking groups, engaging with other attendees and exchanging contact information.
- Develop a strong online presence using platforms such as LinkedIn, Twitter, or industry-specific forums to connect with professionals in your field.

Networking Etiquette: Making a Positive Impression

When networking, it's essential to make a positive and lasting impression. Consider these networking etiquette tips:

- Be genuine, authentic, and approachable, showing genuine interest in others and listening attentively to their stories or perspectives.
- Offer value to your connections, sharing your knowledge, expertise, or resources and demonstrating your willingness to help or support them.
- Follow up promptly and consistently, expressing your gratitude for their time and continuing to nurture your relationship through regular communication and engagement.

The Art of Building Meaningful Relationships

To build meaningful and lasting professional relationships, consider adopting the following practices:

- Invest time and effort in getting to know your connections, understanding their needs, goals, and interests, and identifying areas of mutual benefit or collaboration.

- Provide regular updates, sharing news, achievements, or insights that may be of interest or value to your connections.
- Be responsive and reliable, promptly answering inquiries or requests and delivering on your promises or commitments.

Leveraging Your Network for Business Growth

Your professional network can be a powerful resource for driving your business's growth and success. To leverage your network effectively, consider the following:

- Seeking advice or mentorship from experienced entrepreneurs, industry experts, or peers who can provide valuable guidance, feedback, or support.
- Identifying potential customers, suppliers, investors, or partners within your network and reaching out to explore opportunities for collaboration or business development.
- Harnessing the power of word-of-mouth marketing, asking your connections to refer, endorse, or recommend your products, services, or brand to their networks.

Expanding Your Network: Diversifying and Strengthening Your Connections

To ensure your network remains diverse, dynamic, and relevant, consider:

- Continuously seeking new connections, attending events, joining professional organizations, or participating in online forums and groups.
- Actively nurturing relationships with individuals from different industries, backgrounds, or roles, broadening your perspective, and enhancing your learning opportunities.

- Periodically review and update your network, identifying gaps or areas for growth and prioritizing your networking efforts accordingly.

In conclusion, mastering the art of networking can significantly enhance your entrepreneurial journey, providing valuable resources, insights, and opportunities to drive your business's growth and success. By following the strategies and recommendations outlined in this bonus chapter, you can build, maintain, and leverage a powerful professional network that supports and enriches your entrepreneurial endeavors.

Example Business Plan:

Executive Summary

Business Name: GreenBite Deli

Overview: GreenBite Deli is a fast-casual, eco-friendly restaurant that focuses on providing fresh, healthy, and sustainable food options in a convenient, modern setting. Located downtown, GreenBite Deli aims to cater to the growing demand for healthier food options among busy professionals, students, and residents.

Mission: To create a positive impact on our community and the environment by offering delicious, nutritious, and eco-friendly food choices in a welcoming and sustainable atmosphere.

Objectives:

- Become a go-to destination for healthy and sustainable food options in the downtown area.
- Achieve a monthly revenue of $30,000 within the first year of operation.
- Expand to at least two additional locations within five years.

- Establish a strong brand presence, both online and offline that is synonymous with quality, health, and sustainability.

Company Ownership: GreenBite Deli will be a privately-owned business, with equal shares held by Jane Doe and John Smith, who bring their combined experience in the food and hospitality industries.

Products and Services: GreenBite Deli will offer a variety of sandwiches, salads, wraps, and smoothies made from fresh, locally-sourced ingredients. Vegan, vegetarian, and gluten-free options will be available to accommodate various dietary preferences. The menu will be updated seasonally to ensure the use of fresh, in-season ingredients.

Market Analysis: With the increasing awareness of health and environmental issues, the demand for healthy and eco-friendly food options is on the rise. GreenBite Deli will target health-conscious consumers, including busy professionals, students, and residents of the downtown area who are seeking convenient and nutritious meal options. By positioning ourselves in a prime downtown location, we will be accessible to a large portion of our target market.

Marketing Strategy: Our marketing efforts will focus on creating awareness about our unique offerings and building a strong brand identity. We will implement a combination of digital marketing campaigns, local advertising, and strategic partnerships with local businesses and influencers. We will also encourage customer loyalty through a rewards program and special promotions.

Operations Plan: GreenBite Deli will operate seven days a week, from 7:00 am to 8:00 pm on weekdays and from 9:00 am to 6:00 pm on weekends. We will employ a team of 10-12 staff members, including a full-time manager, kitchen staff, and service staff. The restaurant will have a seating capacity of 40-50 customers.

Management Team: Jane Doe has over 10 years of experience in the hospitality industry, including restaurant management, marketing, and customer service. John Smith is a trained chef with 8 years of experience in various upscale restaurants, specializing in healthy and sustainable cuisine.

Financial Projections: We expect GreenBite Deli to achieve a positive cash flow by the end of the first year, with projected revenues of $360,000 and expenses of $310,000. The initial investment required to start the business is estimated at $150,000, which will cover leasehold improvements, equipment, inventory, and working capital.

Risk Assessment: Potential risks include increased competition, fluctuations in food prices, and changes in consumer preferences. We will mitigate these risks by continuously monitoring market trends, maintaining strong relationships with suppliers, and adapting our menu and marketing strategies as needed.

In conclusion, GreenBite Deli aims to capitalize on the growing demand for healthy and eco-friendly food options by providing fresh, delicious, and sustainable meal choices in a convenient and modern setting. With a strong management team, a comprehensive marketing strategy, and a commitment to quality and sustainability, GreenBite Deli is poised for success in the fast-casual restaurant market.

414 Industries Online Courses

We never stop learning. Check out other books by Jules Beshears and 414 Industries

https://amzn.to/3xib4Ph Checkout our books on amazon

https://414industries.com/

https://www.instagram.com/414industries/

https://www.facebook.com/414industries

www.ingramcontent.com/pod-product-compliance
Lightning Source LLC
Chambersburg PA
CBHW070756220526
45467CB00014B/645